Learning Legacies:
A Guide to Family Learning

Acknowledgements

I want to thank my families and friends – on both sides of the Atlantic – for first-hand experience of learning in families!

Many people have had a hand in producing this Guide. Titus Alexander made a significant contribution to the research and writing of Part 1, for which I am grateful. All of my colleagues at NIACE have played a part through their good humour and practical help. The NIACE Family Learning Advisory Group was a source of wit and wisdom.

To all the families, tutors, managers and supporters who shared their practice with me, I am most grateful. You have been, and continue to be, an inspiration!

NIACE would like to thank the Lloyds TSB Foundation for its generous support in funding the research and its dissemination.

Introduction

Since the publication of *Riches Beyond Price* (Alexander and Clyne, 1995), the concept of family learning has become well established. Government ministers frequently refer to its importance, there is an annual family learning weekend at the start of October, Adult Learners' Week has a family learning award and new initiatives appear all the time. Many local authorities, schools, health authorities and other agencies have established posts, projects and programmes to support family learning. Funding is available through central and local government as well as the National Lottery and charitable trusts. In place of the 'ragged patchwork' described in *Riches Beyond Price*, there are now some vibrant patterns emerging across the country.

These patterns, however, are somewhat uneven in coverage and definition. There are in some areas exquisitely detailed motifs, but in others the effect is rather broad-brushed. There is as yet no commonly accepted definition of family learning and the overall picture is not yet clear for all to see.

This Guide aims to provide a practical and comprehensive overview for parents and professionals wanting to support family learning at any level – community, local, regional or national. It highlights examples of interesting and good practice which contribute to the rich picture of family learning today.

Part 1 sets out the case for family learning today – what family learning means and why it matters in contemporary society. Part 2 describes different approaches to family learning, drawing on notions of a family 'life cycle'. Part 3 discusses operational and strategic matters which contribute to good practice. An opportunity to take stock and look ahead forms the conclusion in Part 4.

The canvas of family learning is unfinished but full of energy and colour! There is enormous scope for families, professionals and policy-makers to make their marks upon the canvas. NIACE hopes this Guide will help you to make an impact.

Part I

The case for family learning

Chapter 1 defines family learning and explains the fundamental principles underpinning it. Chapter 2 explains why family learning matters by looking at the evidence of recent research and the current context in which it is developing.

Learning in the kitchen *(Fela Adebiyi)*

I

What is family learning?

This chapter:

▶ defines family learning;
▶ identifies five major types of family learning;
▶ makes clear some important underlying assumptions about family learning.

Types of family learning

Family learning means, first and foremost, learning which takes place among family members – the complex, sometimes confusing, occasionally damaging, patterns of behaviour, thought and feeling developed within family life.

In practice, 'family learning' is often used as a shorthand for what people outside the family do to enable and facilitate the learning that goes on in families. This Guide uses a practical definition of support for family learning based on *Riches Beyond Price* (Alexander and Clyne, 1995) and taken up by the Campaign for Learning and many local authorities. This definition identified 'five distinct aspects of family learning:

▶ informal learning within the family;
▶ family members learning together;
▶ learning about roles, relationships and responsibilities in relation to the stages of family life, including parenting education;

▶ learning how to understand, take responsibility and make decisions in relation to wider society, in which the family is a foundation for citizenship;

▶ learning how to deal with agencies that serve families.

The common feature of these five aspects is that they involve inter-generational learning based on kinship, however defined.

The importance of this definition is that it is holistic and family-centred. As a broad, all-encompassing term, it emphasises the common ground and connections between different aspects of learning and families. The Campaign for Learning, for example, promotes an inclusive notion of family learning through its annual Family Learning Weekend and by raising awareness of the learning that families do informally in settings as diverse as theme parks and shopping centres.

Gloucestershire LEA has produced a useful, though slightly narrower, definition:

> *'In Family Learning, providers attempt to involve a member/members of a family in learning, which then plays an interactive part in family life, through the transfer, sharing or practising of skills/expertise. It is a process, not just a product.'*

(Family Learning Curriculum Review, 1998)

Oxfordshire County Council's definition of family learning highlights its reciprocal nature and its relationship to everyday family experience:

> *'Family learning involves parents learning either with or through their children and vice versa. Much of family learning is informal and is not recorded in statistics.'*

(Learning Forever, Lifelong Learning Development Plan, 2000–03)

As well as being learners, children and other family members may also take part as educators. It is not uncommon for children to show older adults how to use computers or the internet, while other family members come into school to share their skills and experience.

For practical purposes, providers see family learning in terms of the provision they make for family members to learn, but it is important to remember that all families are places of learning in their own right and all provision for family learning is a partnership.

Clearing the ground

Any discussion of families has to be clear about its underlying assumptions. The following points are worth bearing in mind when planning provision for family learning:

- ▶ first, families are formative influences in people's lives. Whether they are damaging or life-enhancing, families are places of 'deep learning' which touch all aspects of our lives in some way;
- ▶ second, there is no such thing as 'the family', only families. The word 'family' does not just mean one particular type of relationship (married couple with children), but is used as an all-embracing term for inter-generational relationships in which people care for each other;
- ▶ third, families are lifelong relationships, not just about the early years or child-rearing. Families include relationships between older adults and their siblings as well as their grown-up children and other relatives;
- ▶ fourth, parenting is a shared activity that includes responsibilities of fathers as well as mothers, which may in practice be different. There is often an unconscious assumption that 'parenting' means the nurturing, caring aspects of 'mothering', which excludes many of the traditional activities of fathers and also limits the range of things done by mothers;
- ▶ fifth, parenting roles and responsibilities are often shared among several different people, including siblings, grandparents, other relatives, neighbours, childcare workers, teachers and institutions;

▶ sixth, personal relationships, behaviour and attitudes within families vary widely, within and across cultures. There is no one 'right' way to bring up children, and different family traditions have different ways of doing things;

▶ seventh, families and family life are neither good nor bad in themselves. Some are damaging, many are loving, all are places of learning, for good or ill. They happen to be the main social environment into which human beings are born, grow up and live in different ways throughout their lives;

▶ eighth, because families are social environments not institutions, all forms of family learning can affect each other. A family literacy course can trigger much deeper issues involving personal relationships within the family or participation in politics about services for families. Providers need to think about how they can respond positively to wider issues when they arise;

▶ finally, it is important to remember that the first and most influential educators in most children's lives are their parent(s) or carers, particularly in the early years. These can include grandparents, child minders, foster parents, other adults or even an older child.

Family patterns are so diverse that one cannot make any assumptions about who are the significant others in a child's life, nor can one even assume that there is anyone who really cares for each child. But for every child, the presence of at least one loving, caring adult is indispensable. And for parents, the growth of a child into a mature and independent adult can be an important trigger for learning.

Key Points:

▶ families are the formative influences in people's lives and places of 'deep learning';

▶ there is no such thing as 'the family', only families –

intergenerational relationships in which people care for each other;

▶ families and parenting concern men just as much as women – it is a shared activity;

▶ parenting roles and responsibilities are often shared among several different people;

▶ parents and carers are a child's first and most enduring educators;

▶ families are social environments not institutions, in which all forms of learning can affect each other;

▶ personal relationships, behaviour, attitudes and assumptions within families vary widely, within and across cultures;

▶ families and family life are neither good nor bad in themselves. Some families are damaging, many are loving, all are places of learning, for good or ill.

2

Why family learning matters

Learning is part of the social and emotional environment in which children and adults are nurtured in families. This section looks at:

▶ the family's role in promoting learning;
▶ the dynamic relationship between families and social change and how it impacts on this role;
▶ government policy which recognises the significance of family learning.

The family's role in promoting learning

There is ample evidence from medical, social and educational research to demonstrate the importance of the family's role in promoting learning. In particular, research in recent years has led to a greater appreciation of the importance of learning in infancy and early years.

An understanding of how the brain develops provides a neuro-physiological underpinning for family learning. Research on the brain has established its untapped potential for learning (Carter, 1998; Greenfield, 1996). Babies are born with as many brain cells – about 100 billion – as adults, and develop connections through experience and learning from birth. Each nerve cell in the human brain can have tens of thousands of links with other cells, giving every human brain immense capacity to store information. Estimates of how much brain capacity we use varies from 2% to 25% at most. This research highlights the untapped potential for informal learning in and around the home.

The relationship between emotional and cognitive learning is highlighted by Goleman (1996):

> *'Family life is our first school for emotional learning; in this intimate cauldron we learn how to feel about ourselves and how others will react to our feelings.'*

Positive parenting contributes to a sense of emotional safety for learning, enabling young children to explore their world confidently. The process of storing memories means that the context, association or environment in which something is experienced also affects the way in which it is recalled. If the event or fact is emotionally charged in any way, it will be stored so that it will be recalled vividly with its pleasant or unpleasant associations. Emotions and moods therefore have a powerful influence on how we learn and remember.

The importance of families in raising educational attainment is now well established (for a review see Wolfendale and Bastiani, 2000). Sharing books with babies as young as 7 months has been shown to raise children's attainment in Key Stage 1 SATs at 7 and 8 years (Wade and Moore, 2000). Low level of parental interest in education was shown to correlate with poor basic skills (Parsons and Bynner, 2000), as was low literacy scores of parents (Adult Literacy and Basic Skills Unit, 1993).

The provision of Family Literacy and Family Numeracy programmes has been shown to reverse this link. Evaluation of programmes (Brooks *et al*, 1996; Brooks *et al*, 1997; Basic Skills Agency, 1998) shows that there are benefits in terms of:

- ▶ parents' own basic skills;
- ▶ parents' ability to help their children;
- ▶ young children's acquisition of literacy and numeracy;
- ▶ the likelihood of families engaging in literacy and numeracy-related activities in the home.

Family literacy programmes for Urdu- and Punjabi-speaking families delivered similar benefits (Brooks *et al*, 1999).

Research on black adult high-achievers from low income backgrounds identified 'family success factors' such as attitudes towards work, feelings of competence and hard work (Clark, 1983). Particularly important was 'a family dream of success for the future. Parents have a vision of success for each child and talk with children about steps to realise this vision.' The researchers suggest these factors cut across family income, education and ethnic background.

Taken together, there is overwhelming evidence to demonstrate the contribution of learning in families to the emotional, cognitive and social development of individual members, particularly in the critical phase of early brain development.

The dynamic relationship between changing families and social change

There are many graphic ways of describing the sense of breathless social change that we are experiencing now. 'Dream time' is how storytellers in some cultures depict transitional times (Ramsay, 2000). The one certainty is that change is constant. Families, as social institutions, are always changing as shifts in the economy and changes in social attitudes wash around them.

One of the major areas affecting families today is the changing nature of work. The relationship between labour market trends and family life is well researched. Evidence (Dex, 1999; Warin *et al*, 1999) reveals:

▶ greater polarisation between the dual-earner and no-earner households;
▶ a culture of long working hours which impacts on contact time available for the family;
▶ tension in the demand for fathers to be both 'providers' and 'emotionally involved';
▶ more women in the labour market.

Moreover, the notion of a 'job for life' has gone, making work-place changes more frequent and responsibility for re-training an individual matter.

The gap between those who benefit from employment and those who do not is widening (Dex, 1999). A significant number of children and their families are living in conditions of poverty. Poverty is a major factor in social exclusion, but not the only one. Families may also experience a lack of influence in matters which affect their well-being and a sense of powerlessness (Thompson, 2000). Children growing up in such families may feel that education has nothing to offer them and begin to dis-engage.

Families too have been changing over the past decades. Families break down more frequently now, though serial mar-riages contribute to a growing number of step-families (Dex, 1999). Children of divorced or separated parents may have experience of living between two families. Families headed by a lone parent are likely to rely on networks of family and friends for support.

Dex (1999) observes that a striking feature of cultural change is our celebration of individualism and emphasis on per-sonal choice, which is encouraging looser social networks. For families with employment and a reasonable standard of living this may be a welcome change, but for families experiencing material hardship this may add to a sense of alienation.

There is evidence that family and community learning can encourage individuals to remain active in social and economic life. McGivney (2000) found that parents in disadvantaged neighbourhoods who were involved in pre-school playgroups reported that benefits included the confidence to seek employ-ment and aspire towards higher goals. Parents wanting to sup-port their children in learning may also be motivated to undertake learning for their own benefit (McGivney, 2000).

OECD research (1999) cited the example of Priory Primary School in Dudley as a model for addressing social exclusion. The school serves an estate characterised by multiple depriva-tion, as evidenced in the high rate of long-term unemployment and higher than average rate of free school meals. In 1993 a new headteacher launched the Priory Partnership Project to raise pupil achievement by involving parents in their children's learning. The research documents the wider benefits of the partnership in terms of the whole community's involvement and raised aspirations. The research notes that 'community and individual benefits came in equal measure from the work'. Furthermore,

> *'Long-standing patterns have been broken at Priory Primary, to create a virtuous rather than vicious circle. The route to community school status, with a fully-fledged adult education service, may have been a serendipitous outcome of efforts to raise pupil standards, but it is all the better for that and is a model that is worth closer attention.'*

The preliminary evidence (Pascal *et al*, 1999) from the evaluation of 8 of the 29 Early Excellence Centres suggests that they can break cycles of deprivation by building trust, mutuality and understanding, which empowers parents to develop their abilities as parents and become more active participants in the local community.

Overall, there is a body of important evidence of the contribution that family learning makes to social inclusion and community regeneration.

Government policy on family learning

Family learning is part of a wider raft of family-related policies and initiatives, all of which indicate the importance which the Government attaches to this area:

▶ the white paper *Learning to Succeed* (1999) states that 'community, adult and family learning will be essential in the Learning Age';

▶ the report of the Moser Committee on adult basic skills (DfEE, 1999b) notes that family literacy and numeracy programmes 'help to prevent early failure in young children and improve the the literacy and numeracy skills of adults';

- ▶ *Excellence in Schools* (1997) stresses the importance of schools and parents working together to raise standards;
- ▶ *Meeting the Childcare Challenge* (1998) announces the Government's intention to develop a national childcare strategy;
- ▶ a report by the Schools Plus Policy Action Team (2000) recommends extension of the school into the community and of involving parents and community in the school to combat social exclusion;
- ▶ publications by the Social Exclusion Unit focus on neighbourhood strategies, including Sure Start, the programme for early intervention to ensure children go to school ready to learn;
- ▶ *Supporting Families* (DoH, 1998) sets out the Government's vision of how better to support families and respond to crises if appropriate.

The sheer the number of separate initiatives and the range of departments involved makes the co-ordination of family learning difficult.

A significant contribution has been the Ofsted (2000) report, *Family Learning: a Survey of Current Practice*. While the survey uses a narrower definition of family learning than that used generally, it nonetheless sets out an important agenda for action, which recommends that:

- ▶ **institutions** devise strategies for assessing joint learning and for staff development;
- ▶ **local authorities** incorporate family learning into the full range of its priorities, not just raising achievement; develop a policy framework; develop outreach strategies; improve quality assurance; consider earmarked funding; and check on the value for money of provision;
- ▶ **national government** ends short-term funding; considers central funding to stimulate a wider curriculum; encourages more long-term evaluation of the benefits of family learning.

The report is significant in locating family learning within the context of social inclusion and lifelong learning priorities.

Overall, the Government's recognition of the significance of the family as a context for learning is clear, even if the overarching vision is not.

Key Points:

▶ brain connections develop rapidly in the early years, creating emotional and cognitive capacities for learning;

▶ parenting influences a child's well-being and life chances;

▶ parental involvement in children's education raises attainment at school;

▶ learning in families can act as trigger to lifelong learning and participation in the community;

▶ it is in the national interest to invest in parenting and family life because of the contribution families make to the economic and social wealth;

▶ family learning can help people to deal with change and uncertainty in contemporary society.

Part 2

Approaches to
family learning

This section examines different approaches to family learning. Two motifs run through the approaches taken as a whole. First is the motif of a family 'life cycle': that is, a sequence of stages which most families encounter, though each family will experience the stages in unique ways. Second is the motif of the family's interaction with other dominant social structures such as schooling and employment.

The approaches and motifs are presented as a way of highlighting patterns in the otherwise crowded canvas of family learning.

melani

Daddy is '12'

melanie is '4'

'This is my family' by Melanie (4 years old) (*Jesmond Nursery Ltd, Newcastle Upon Tyne*)

3

Parenting education

Introduction

Parenting education and support is a wide-ranging category of family learning which includes many different models. This chapter looks at some of the key features and models of parenting education.

What is parenting education?

Parenting education and support 'includes a range of education and support measures which:

▶ help parents and prospective parents to understand their own social, emotional, psychological and physical needs and those of their children and enhance the relationship between them; and

▶ create a supportive network of services with local communities and help families to take advantage of them' (Pugh *et al*, 1994).

Parenting education and support is characterised by a core set of beliefs which value parents, children and parenting. In developing programmes or forming parenting education networks, facilitators generally make these beliefs explicit, as parents and providers in Plymouth do in the following example.

The Plymouth principles for parenting education and support services

Parents and providers attending a parenting conference in Plymouth recently identified the principles which underpin quality work:

▶ importance of parenting in shaping children's lives;
▶ parents valued and respected;
▶ recognition of cultural diversity;
▶ no blueprint for best parenting;
▶ parenting influenced by range of circumstances;
▶ services should respond to parents' needs;
▶ services should be non-stigmatising.

(Parenting in Plymouth, 2000)

Parenting education and support is provided by a range of local authority departments and agencies in the voluntary sector, frequently in collaboration. It features in many Sure Start programmes and Early Excellence Centres. Because it is generally informal and person-centred, it can serve as a first step to learning for parents, who frequently gain the confidence to become group facilitators themselves.

Parenting education and support models

There are many different models of parenting education and support, including:

▶ group-based parenting education programmes;
▶ family life education in schools and centres;
▶ preparation and support for parenthood;
▶ telephone helpline services;
▶ issue-related work targeting particular groups of parents, eg, men, ethnic minority communities.

Group-based programmes

Group-based parenting education programmes are open to all parents rather than a targeted group. Parents attend a planned course which generally covers:

▶ communicating with and building a good relationship with children;
▶ encouraging appropriate behaviour;
▶ looking after parents' own needs.

The Open University's 'Confident Parents, Confident Children' and the Pre-School Learning Alliance's 'Looking at Learning Together' are examples of group-based programmes.

Facilitators employ groupwork techniques to put parents at their ease and generate an open, trusting climate, similar to that found in effective families. Programmes may be short and non-accredited or accredited. Either way, in enhancing parents' confidence, they often lead to further learning opportunities.

Family life education

These opportunities aim to develop an understanding of family life and skills in taking part in families. These aims are pursued through a number of innovative strategies involving some or all of the family.

The case studies on page 20 illustrate two approaches to family life education.

Preparation for parenthood

Parenting is a major undertaking. These programmes aim to help parents deal with the transition to parenthood, either through antenatal or postnatal provision. Homestart is a national agency which offers help to families with at least one child under the age of five who are experiencing stress

YMCA and Care for the Family
'Dads and Lads – For Fathers and Men Who Care'

This project aims to help fathers and mentors become better role models and boys make the transition to adulthood more successfully. It uses sport to enhance positive interaction and communication between fathers and their sons. Rather than 'watch from the sidelines', dads are encouraged to participate in team games which develop transferable skills which can enhance family life. Important skills include working as part of a team, building confidence and self-esteem, and having fun together. A high quality magazine entitled 'DAD' forms the basis of a parenting course for fathers.

(Source of funding: Home Office)

Kent Children's University, Residential Weekend

Kent Children's University aims to provide residential learning for families with young children who may be experiencing stress. Families spend a weekend at the local authority's outdoor education centre, a large residence in spacious grounds. Over the weekend they engage in a varied programme of activities, including outdoor pursuits, team exercises, producing a newspaper, storytelling, and enjoying meal times together in the large dining room.

These are experiences which many families would not ordinarily have. Staff help parents and children to reflect on their new experience and to talk about its meanings. While a weekend is not enough time to consolidate complex skills, staff aim to bring families together to share new experiences and to start them thinking in new ways about them. Follow-up work after the residential weekend aims to consolidate some of the learning.

(Source of funding: Adult and Community Learning Fund)

or difficulties. It provides a 'befriending service' in which an experienced parent will visit the home and devise a support programme customised to the family's needs.

Where a family has a child with a disability, support can be especially welcomed. Contact a Family is a national charity which provides support to families who care for children with any disability or special need. The services it offers include:

▶ a telephone helpline;
▶ local parent support groups;
▶ national support networks;
▶ one-to-one support;
▶ a quarterly newsletter and a directory of rare conditions;
▶ liaison with other professionals.

They support a team of local volunteers, all parents themselves of children with disabilities, who are trained to signpost other parents and professional workers to local sources of help. Contact a Family's support for local groups and volunteer representatives are good examples of building capacity amongst parents to tackle important family issues.

Telephone helpline

Many parents can benefit from sound information, advice and guidance provided over the telephone. Parentline Plus is a new organisation formed following the amalgamation of Parentline and the National Stepfamily Association. Its national free-phone helpline offers confidential support and information to anyone in a parenting role. It provides training to volunteer parents to enable them to advise callers on a range of issues, from straightforward requests for information to more difficult family dilemmas. Support is also available through publications and professional development.

Issue-based programmes for particular groups of parents

Some groups of parents have particular needs which are best addressed through issue-based programmes. Fathers, parents of teenagers, lone parents, teenage parents, black and ethnic minority parents, and parents of children in trouble are examples of particular groups which are targeted through specialised programmes.

Parents of children at risk of disaffection from school, for example, can be supported through INCLUDE, a national charity funded by the Home Office which provides one-to-one help in developing behaviour management strategies. INCLUDE advisers liaise between the school and home to improve communication and understanding on both sides.

Youth Offending Teams (YOTs) are funded by the Home Office to work with parents whose children have offended to improve their strategies for dealing with relationships. In the Sunderland pilot YOT, the Let's Talk programme adopts an empowerment model which aims to restore parents' confidence to manage difficult situations.

Key Points:

▶ parenting education and support is a wide-ranging category of family learning which includes many different learning models;

▶ the focus is on the skills and understanding involved in parenting and living in families;

▶ programmes subscribe to a view of parents and children as valued members of society for whom learning builds individual and collective capacity for relationships.

4

Pre-school family learning

Introduction

In the years before formal schooling begins, babies and young children are learning about their world through active exploration and play. During this period parents are learning about their children's and their own needs and capabilities. This section looks at some of the ways of supporting this rich period of mutual discovery, including:

▶ learning in the home;
▶ integrated family services;
▶ community-based learning.

Learning in the home

The home is a very powerful environment for learning. In most ways it is significantly more powerful than the learning environment children will encounter when they begin school. Some significant features of home learning as opposed to school learning (Hannon, 1995) are that it:

▶ is more spontaneous than school learning;
▶ includes extended conversations;
▶ features a much higher adult-child ratio than school learning;

- features close and continuous relationships rather than distant and discontinuous relationships;
- is shaped by the child's interests and needs;
- has a flexible rather than fixed duration.

Of course not every home offers all these advantages to the same degree. Whatever the pressures on home, though, the fact remains that it is a distinctive learning environment with great potential for helping babies and young children to learn. Moreover, the learning achievements from this period are quite remarkable – using language, walking, and relating to people.

Sure Start is a major government programme that has as one of its aims improving the ability to learn in children 0-4 years of age. It will do this 'by encouraging stimulating and enjoyable play, improving language skills and through early identification and support of children with language difficulties' (DfEE, 1999c). Home visiting by health visitors is one of the core services specified in the Sure Start guidelines. Another national programme which supports family learning in the home, Bookstart (see case study, page 25), focuses on early sharing of books.

Programmes which help families to maximise the potential of the home for learning are an important form of support for families.

Integrated family services

Integrated family service models offer a range of services to meet all of the family's needs, including their learning needs. The family centre is one way of delivering integrated services. The Pen Green Centre for under 5s and their families in Corby, described on page 26, is a leader in this field.

(Pen Green Centre's programme for adult learning with progression to training and employment opportunities is described further in Chapter 6)

Bookstart – sharing books in the home

Bookstart is a national programme sponsored by Sainsbury's and supported by the National Book Trust. The aim is to encourage early book sharing by parents and babies. Research has shown that the experience of book sharing is related to enhanced literacy development in babies. Babies who experienced book sharing went on to achieve higher SATs results seven years later than a control group of children who had no such experience. Interestingly they performed better in both English and maths tests.

Libraries and health visitors collaborate to get the message of book sharing to parents. Parents receive a free bag containing a baby book when they attend the health clinic for the babies' seven months health check. The bags also include information about how to join the library. Many local libraries have provided community-based learning activities such as storysack groups in local libraries to follow-up the health visitors' work. Library membership has also gone up in some cases.

(Source of funding: Sainsbury's and local authorities)

Another model for working with families in the community is that of the Pre-School Learning Alliance (PSLA), a national body promoting education and care for under-fives in England. 80 per cent of pre-school groups in the country are affiliated to the PSLA, which supports 18,000 member groups meeting the needs of about 850,000 children and their families (McGivney, 2000).

The PSLA uses a community development approach, working alongside other organisations at neighbourhood level. Parents are encouraged to take an active role in running and managing groups, and in doing so gain skills and understanding in child development and community work. Research into the benefits for parents in areas of social and economic disadvantage of involvement in pre-school playgroups highlights their role in promoting family learning (see Figure 1 on page 27).

Pen Green Centre for under 5s and their families – 'a one stop shop'

The Pen Green Centre in Corby is a model for the government's Early Excellence Centres (EEC). EECs are part of the government's strategy for tackling a raft of social objectives relating to education, health, neighbourhood renewal and poverty through integrated approaches. EECs offer a range of services for children, their families and the community.

Pen Green is a pioneer of integrated services, established in 1983 through collaboration of the LEA, Social Services Department and the Area Health Authority. From the outset it involved the whole community in determining services and managing the centre. The services offered include:

► high quality education and care;
► adult and community education;
► family support services;
► community regeneration;
► child and family health service;
► training and research.

The Centre's vision of learning includes families learning together as well as individual learning – in fact, the Pen Green vision asserts that parents' and children's learning are strongly entwined:

> 'What we are aiming to offer children at the Centre, we also want to offer to parents and staff. We see the Centre's role as enabling personal growth, development and learning, the enjoyment that comes with friendships, time to be active and time to reflect, to listen and be listened to... Time spent at the Centre is not about working through a programme or to reach a goal. We all have different starting lines, whether child, parent or staff and there is no winning post or race to be won.'

(Pen Green Centre for under 5s and their Families, n.d.)

(Sources of Funding: a package which includes funding from the LEA, FEFC, SRB, ESF, Homestart, National Lottery, and DfEE for Sure Start and Early Excellence Centre.)

Figure 1 – The benefits to parents of involvement in pre-school playgroups

- ▶ New social contacts
- ▶ New activities with children at home
- ▶ Involvement with local schools
- ▶ Co-operative and self-help activities with other parents
- ▶ Participation in education and training
- ▶ Setting up events/activities for children
- ▶ Sought/obtained employment
- ▶ Membership of other local group/organisations
- ▶ Community activism (bringing about local changes)
- ▶ Found a job would not have previously thought could do

McGivney, 2000

Pre-school playgroups based on a community development model promoting family learning are 'a vital family and community resource in socially and economically disadvantaged areas' (McGivney, 2000).

These two models of integrated family services represent a major step forward in family learning involving pre-school children.

Community-based family learning services

There are many other community-based services which support family learning – museums, galleries, libraries, parks, and leisure centres, to name but a few. 'Engage', the national association for gallery education, for example, is targeting primary school children and their parents through a programme called 'encompass'. The exhibitions it supports target families, for example those from ethnic minority communities, which have traditionally not used galleries. New 'Centres for curiosity and imagination' aim to stimulate and support the development of creativity for children and families throughout the UK. These centres will:

- ▶ help children to understand themselves, other people and the world around them;
- ▶ foster qualities such as curiosity, creativity and self-esteem;
- ▶ provide playful hands-on exhibitions;
- ▶ support the role of parents and carers;
- ▶ respond to the needs of the local community;
- ▶ provide maximum access.

Libraries have always served families, and in many neighbour-hoods they are seen as the least threatening of the statutory services. The case study on page 29 demonstrates how libraries are developing new approaches to reach particular groups of readers, in this case fathers and sons.

Pre-school family services tend to focus on the family as a unit, and in this respect they have developed good practice in family learning from which other can learn.

Key Points:

- ▶ the home is a distinctive, and potentially rich, environment for family learning, now benefiting from new resources through the Government's Sure Start programme;
- ▶ family centres with integrated services have established good practice in promoting family learning;
- ▶ community-based services such as pre-school playgroups, libraries, galleries, museums and leisure services are adopting a range of innovative strategies for reaching families.

Lancashire County Council Library Services
Dads and Lads Programme

The Dads and Lads programme was devised by Lancashire Library and its partners to encourage fathers to read with their pre-school sons. Family learning programmes attract predominantly women, so the under-representation of fathers and male carers was one concern. Librarians and parental involvement workers were also aware of boys' under-achievement in reading and difficulty in developing fine motor control which enables them to develop writing skills. The Dads and Lads programme sought to tackle these issues through a family learning approach.

They knew from research that men favour active learning and competition. Adapting a scheme called Top Tots from the Sports Council, they made rucksacks which were sent home with boys in participating nursery schools. The rucksacks contained a different storybook and piece of PE equipment each week. At home the dads organised play activities with the sports equipment and reading sessions with the relevant story and a short action poem. The humorous books were specially selected to match the sporting theme.

The scheme culminated in a grand competition at Burnley Football Club, where 100 dads and their sons played games and answered questions on the books they had read. The winning team was awarded a prize cup, watched by partners and siblings. The programme, running over six weeks, targeted areas where literacy was under-developed.

(Source of Funding: Lancashire County Library and
Lancashire Adult and Continuing Education Service)

Encouraging lifelong learning *(Nick Hayes)*

5

Home-school partnerships

This section examines the notion of 'partnership' between parents and schools and describes some of the practical strategies for working together.

What forms does partnership take?

Ball (1998) devised a useful framework for thinking about the different types of relationships between the school, family and community (see Table 1 on page 32).

Fundamental issues

The notion of partnership is now fundamental to any consideration of home-school relationships. It has developed from a number of key government agenda, such as seeing parents as consumers, clarifying the roles and responsibilities of parents and schools, and enlisting parents' help in raising standards.

At the same time, the notion of partnership inevitably raises fundamental issues which must be addressed, including:

Table 1 – Types of Home-School Community Relationships

1. Decision-making and management, for example, through parent governors
2. Communication between home and school, for example, reports and letters about children's progress
3. School support for families, for example, relating to health and behaviour
4. Family and community help for schools, for example, where parents help out in the classroom
5. School support for learning at home, for example, school initiatives to promote learning at home
6. Collaborations with community agencies, for example, local and national agencies support the school
7. Community education, for example, providing learning opportunities for everyone in the community

(Ball, 1998)

▶ the balance of power. Professionals have more power than parents, and unless strategies are devised to enable parents to share power, the partnership will be tokenistic;

▶ the diversity of families. Schools may have in mind an 'ideal family' which excludes many of the very families they might say they want to reach;

▶ the culture of the school. Links with the family and community may be bolted on to what the school sees as its core business, educational achievement. They need to be embedded in the values, beliefs and everyday practices of the school.

A genuine notion of partnership is based on:

▶ sharing power;
▶ taking positive action to include all families;
▶ a whole-school approach to partnership.

Home-school agreements: introducing 'dialogue'

Home-school links are now formalised through mandatory home-school agreements, which set out the roles and responsibilities of schools and parents and the expectations of pupils. Governors must consult all parents about them, take all reasonable steps to get everyone signed up, and review them from time to time.

The 'dialogue game' is used in schools to begin the discussion on roles and responsibilities of parents and schools. The game gets governors, parents, teachers and other staff to debate a series of statements about what can be expected of pupils of a certain age. Participants must decide who is responsible for the child in that instance – parents or the school? A frequent reaction is that most items are the joint responsibility of parents and school.

Partnership structures

Liverpool's Parent School Partnership, described on page 34, illustrates a well established approach to joint working between the schools, parents and the local authority.

Home-school links and minority ethnic groups

Some ethnic minority communities establish supplementary or mother-tongue schools to maintain language, culture and identity. These have strong support from parents who value education and see the schools as a focus for their community. It is estimated that there are about 400 schools of this kind in London alone (Ball, 1998). The links between supplementary schools and state schools are developing in some cities.

In Nottingham a different approach, described on page 35, is being used to reach ethnic minority communities through a project known as 'AMBER'.

The Liverpool Parent School Partnership

The Liverpool Parent School Partnership (PSP) provides a city-wide service free of charge to all schools by a development team in the Community and Continuing Education Service. Parental involvement in education is an integral part of Liverpool's Community Education Policy.

Liverpool has a detailed statement of practice, principles and aims, as well as Guidelines for Involving Parents in Education and Guidelines for Involving Parents Who Have Basic Skills Needs. The Partnership's provision in schools serves as an access route through the 'REACHOut™ to Parents' Programme which can take learners from informal non-accredited work up to degree level. The partnership has attracted major funding from regeneration programmes and private sponsors alike.

By having a dedicated team of home-school development officers, the city's provision has developed into well-defined progression routes accredited through the Open College Network. Parents who have benefited stay involved at community level as facilitators and contribute to a curriculum development group.

(Source of funding: a package of funding from the local authority, SRB, the private sector and Liverpool Hope University)

Support for families during transitions

Transitions are recognised as especially important times in a child's school career. Parents are now routinely involved in transitions from nursery to primary and from primary to secondary phases. The London Borough of Enfield is also involving families in thinking about the transition from school to university (see case study, page 36).

Parental involvement in schools, widely promoted through home-school partnership, is a well developed practice with a growing evidence base (Wolfendale and Bastiani, 2000). Extending good practice to include all parents and communities, however, remains a challenge.

AMBER – 'Adult Minorities Breaking Educational Restrictions'

AMBER aims to:

▶ improve the understanding of Asian and African-Caribbean parents of the education system and the curriculum so they can support their children;

▶ develop the understanding of schools of the needs and contributions of Asian and African-Caribbean parents and their children;

▶ develop communication between home and school to minimise risk of exclusion;

▶ provide English language, literacy and numeracy skills for parents where necessary;

▶ provide educational guidance and vocational guidance for Asian and African-Caribbean parents;

▶ educate/train Asian and African-Caribbean adults to work as Parent Education Support Workers, with opportunities to progress to further and higher education or employment opportunities. (Bastiani, 2000a)

The project, established in 1995, is a partnership involving New College Nottingham, Nottingham Black Initiative and local schools.

It created 24 new Parent Education Support Worker (PESW) posts, placed in schools with a high proportion of ethnic minority children. Workers serve as both catalysts in schools and role models for the community. They are the link between the work of schools and the needs and concerns of families. AMBER's achievements include:

▶ enhanced parent participation in the school, including parents' evenings;

▶ parents enrolling on further education courses;

▶ parents becoming school governors;

▶ PESW training in a wide range of areas.

(Source of funding: Ethnic Minority Achievement Grant (Home Office), FEFC, Nottingham Black Initiative, New College Nottingham, and the Adult and Community Learning Fund.)

London Borough of Enfield: UCAS support programme

Transitions for individual family members often require efforts from the family as a whole. Enfield LEA believes that lifelong learning begins at birth and continues throughout life. Each phase of schooling is a staging post along the way, and transitions from one phase to the next are like the handing-on of a baton in a relay race. Each phase of education must take responsibility to prepare families for the next phase.

The UCAS support programme aims to raise aspirations of students for higher education and to help their families to support them in getting there. There are four strands to the programme:

1. introductory HE briefings at Key Stage 4 for every student involving local universities;
2. support sessions late in Year 12 to help students complete their UCAS form;
3. a series of school-based family learning evenings which deals with preparing for A level success and entry to university, staged early in Year 13 for parents;
4. a one-day university pre-induction programme for every aspiring university student late in year 13.

By supporting the whole family during this key transitional phase, Enfield LEA hopes to encourage more students to aspire to higher education and to realise their ambitions. In turn, families' knowledge of higher education is enhanced, with benefits for the community at large.

(Source of funding: DfEE Standards Funds, Lifelong Learning)

Key Points:

▶ the idea of a partnership between home and school is promoted by several government agenda;

▶ fundamental questions relating to power and inclusion must be addressed in building partnerships with parents;

▶ opportunities for dialogue should be built into every stage of partnership;

▶ developing partnerships with parents and the community takes time;

▶ the creation of dedicated staff posts enables the development work to be effective;

▶ transition points in learners' lives are times when partnerships with families are critical.

The SEARCH project, Gosport: learning about the past *(Paul Carter)*

6

Family learning at work and in the community

The traditional boundary between the family, workplace and community life is becoming more blurred. No longer are they seen as separate, unrelated spheres. This chapter looks at:

▶ family learning about work;
▶ progression to training and employment opportunities;
▶ employers' support for family learning.

Family attitudes to work

Families are one of the places where people learn attitudes to work. There is evidence that children from families where there is no adult working are more likely to under-perform in school than children from homes where adults are working. Recognising the link between families and vocational aspirations was part of the rationale for an initiative, described on page 40, in which the National Education Business Partnership Network (NEBPN) focused on encouraging parents to support their children's learning.

Family attitudes to work were also the starting point of 'Building Family Learning Units', a European project managed by Warwickshire College. The project focused on the problems faced by women returning to work who fail to complete training courses owing to 'family reasons'. A range of strategies including guidance, counselling and support were targeted at the whole family to build up its capacity to cope with a mother's transition from home to the workplace.

Haringey Education Business Partnership: 'Involving Parents in Compact 2000'

As part of the NEBPN initiative, Haringey EBP focused in part on involving parents for the first time in 'Compact 2000', an agreement between business, schools and the community to work together. As part of the Compact, employers act as mentors to young people in school. The families who took part were those of young people in two mixed comprehensives. The young people were capable, with support, of achieving five GCSEs at grade C or above, but at risk of failing without support.

Young people in Haringey, when interviewed, talked about the importance of family on their aspirations and ability to seek employment. They welcomed parents taking an interest in their studies. 'Making sure that we complete our coursework and homework within deadlines helps us to be responsible and professional,' they said.

Parents were involved by:

▶ meeting with their child's mentor;
▶ identifying what help they needed to support their child's learning;
▶ taking part in the 'employer adoption scheme';
▶ visiting local employers and local college.

Amongst recommendations in the project evaluation are that:

▶ parents with little knowledge or experience of the English education system should be targeted in further work;
▶ opportunities for parents to meet with employers were effective in improving career knowledge.

(Source of Funding: DfEE)

Informal learning as a catalyst for vocational training

Much of family learning is informal in nature, taking place in the home and community. There is now a greater recognition of how this kind of learning serves as a catalyst for formal learning, training and work (McGivney, 1999b, 2000). Family centres are ideally placed to encourage progression from informal learning to formal learning which can lead to qualifications and employment.

One element of the 'full service' offered by Pen Green Centre for under 5s and their families is a programme of informal and formal learning which supports parents when they begin to think of their futures. The first step is often building up the self-esteem of parents who may have failed at school or lost confidence through being at home. Informal learning is promoted by involving parents in their child's care and by providing opportunities for voluntary work in the centre.

The centre also offers a full adult education programme, including non-accredited and accredited courses. There are links with the local college and the centre is an NVQ assessment centre. Many parents become interested in childcare and decide to get qualifications in this area. A 'Wider Opportunities' project supported by the European Social Fund enables unemployed adults to train for employment in childcare. The centre also provides opportunities for paid work which many parents take up.

The route parents take from informal learning to qualifications and employment is rarely straightforward. For parents whose confidence is low this is even less likely. Whalley (1997) illustrates a typical progression route for a parent using the Pen Green Centre (Figure 2).

Figure 2 – Progression from Informal Learning in a Family Centre to Vocational Qualifications

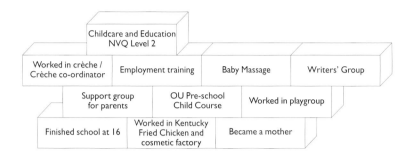

Learner starts here…

(Whalley *et al*, 1997)

Employers' support for family learning

Increasingly employers are realising that family learning makes good sense. Employers who are 'family learning-friendly' are more likely to gain the trust and loyalty of families and the community. This can affect economic performance as well as public relationships. For example, the London Language and Literacy Unit worked with Ford Motors at Dagenham to pilot family numeracy classes, which in turn stimulated demand from employees to improve their basic skills.

The Campaign for Learning's promotion of family learning at work has raised public awareness of the importance of the workplace for all members of the family.

Ford Motors at Dagenham has a varied programme of family learning. Employees and family members over 18 years of age can take advantage of Saturday classes provided as part of the EDAP programme. The Ford Motor Off-line Basic Skills Project, originally funded by the Basic Skills Agency, proved so popular that it is funded now by the company. Non-accredited courses in literacy, numeracy and ICT for parents and children of 7–11 years of age are provided on Saturday mornings. 'Technology for Teenagers' for parents and older children is project-based and meets on Saturday afternoon, a popular time with families. The course draws in a significant proportion of fathers.

British Airways is working in partnership with the London Borough of Hillingdon to develop a Family Learning Centre at the Bell Farm estate. Families spend alternate Saturday afternoons at BA's Community Learning Centre set in a public parkland and nature reserve. The programme develops communication skills, customer services, ICT, marketing and foreign language skills. Activities in the parkland and nature reserve are also part of the curriculum. For BA, family and community learning are part of being a 'good neighbour'.

Key Points:

- family learning can contribute to positive attitudes about employment;
- informal family learning can be the first step of a progression route into training and employment;
- employers can do much to support family learning in the workplace and the community.

Two eclipses in her lifetime: showing her great-grandson how to view safely *(Newcastle Library and Information Service)*

Part 3

Family learning in practice

This part looks at issues relating to practice on the ground and at strategic levels. It is addressed directly to practitioners, to indicate the key issues at each stage rather than detailed procedures.

'Getting started' suggests you can get underway by assessing needs, and over time put effective partnerships and policies in place. 'Funding' addresses key issues in getting the resources to keep your provision going. 'Quality' looks at how to improve your provision once it is up and running.

These three chapters address the central challenge of moving local initiatives from 'good ideas' to sustainable provision that makes a long-term difference.

Father and son talk about learning *(Nick Hayes)*

7

Getting started

Family learning initiatives often begin in small ways, and grow into larger programmes, which in turn stimulate policy-making. You need not wait until a formal policy is in place to begin to work with families. Nor do you need major funding, though once you get to the development stage you will need some resources. Building strong partnerships is a key task along the way. This section looks at this initial phase, including:

▶ assessing need;
▶ developing family learning;
▶ facilitating family learning;
▶ partnerships;
▶ policy.

Assessing need

A good place to start is by assessing the needs of families in your community. You could begin by looking at the learning opportunities you currently provide for family members. This can tell you:

▶ how many family members currently use your provision;
▶ their age and gender;
▶ what they are doing;
▶ where they live;

- ▶ whether they are part of an ethnic minority community;
- ▶ what kind of links you have with other organisations which serve families.

This gives you a picture of how families are currently served by your organisation. You can compare this to a profile of families in your community, using information from, for example:

- ▶ local authority Best Value Reviews;
- ▶ local authority research and information sections;
- ▶ the census;
- ▶ local and regional agencies that work with families.

It is essential to consult families directly about their needs, working through 'gatekeepers' in the community who provide links to families. Families will have clear ideas about what they want. It is important to listen to a range of views and to keep an open mind about what might develop. Making promises too early may lead to disappointment later.

You may also begin to identify different groups of families and family members with particular needs and interests, such as fathers, ethnic minority families, or foster families. Focusing on particular groups enables you to target provision. There is a case for both universal provision from which all families can benefit, as well as targeted opportunities for families that are not coming forward to participate. Reaching these families can be the start of their lifelong learning experience.

You will quickly realise that families are diverse and have a range of learning needs, far too many to be addressed by you and your organisation alone. You will need to prioritise these needs in light of other considerations, for example, your organisation's aims priorities and the other provision in the area.

The Sure Start programme, for example, includes a strong element of consultation with families and the community (see case study, page 49).

Bristol Community Education Service's model of community consultation, described on page 50, has been particularly effective in identifying the needs of families and schools.

Sure Start South East Ipswich
Consultation with the Bangladeshi Community

The aim of this consultation was to ensure that members of the Bangladeshi community in South East Ipswich were aware of, and understood, the Sure Start programme. The Sure Start Steering Group wanted Bangladeshi parents to have a hand in planning new services for families with young children in their community.

A Bangladeshi worker made contact with parents through home visits and encouraged them to attend a group consultation. It was difficult to get parents to attend together as Bangladeshi women generally do not feel comfortable attending meetings with men. However, after negotiations about 30 parents attended and gave their views on what services were needed to improve their children's health and their ability to learn by the time they start school.

As well as the children's services identified, the parents asked for mother tongue language and Arabic classes as a way of attracting more people to the centre and making them feel valued.

(Source of funding: DfEE, Sure Start programme)

Developing learning opportunities

The development stage is critical and one that can easily be underestimated. A surprising amount of time and resources are needed to move forward from ideas to action. If you are applying for new resources, you need to cost the development stage carefully. If you are not getting additional resources, you need to allow more time.

It is important to bring together key stakeholders such as families, tutors, community leaders and staff from other organisations in a planning or steering group. Whatever the scale of the initiative you are developing, whether a small or a large programme, the steps include:

- ▶ programme development, including accreditation where appropriate;
- ▶ materials development if appropriate;
- ▶ piloting the programme;
- ▶ session planning;
- ▶ promoting the programme.

Several national organisations have been instrumental in developing programmes and supporting family learning provision. Accreditation bodies, too, have played an important role by validating programmes enabling parents to gain nationally recognised qualifications. Sources of practical help and the kind of support offered are set out in Table 2 (page 52).

Community Consultation with Parents in Bristol

As part of the New Deal for Communities, Bristol Community Education Service trained parents to consult with the community about what family learning and parental involvement in schools should aim for. One parent researcher discovered that the term 'family learning' aroused negative feelings because:

- ▶ parents did not welcome interference with family life;
- ▶ it was seen as a project for the less able;
- ▶ it was intimidating to parents whose own basic skills were poor.

By asking parents and children to compile a 'wish list' at home, she discovered that what they *really* wanted was 'family projects' around sport, music, art and IT.

The researcher concluded that the request for active projects indicates the need for a wider curriculum than support for children's learning. At the same time, they are valuable 'tools for family learning in their own right, with the facilitator incorporating educational elements as and when appropriate.' (New Deal for Communities Bristol, n.d.)

(Source of Funding: New Deal for Communities)

It is a good idea to pilot your programme so that you can learn from mistakes before finalising it. If you are working up a short programme, the pilot might be a 'taster'. When you have made any adjustments needed, you can promote a programme confidently, using a range of methods, including:

- word of mouth;
- posters, using languages and images appropriate for the community;
- leaflets, distributed through local networks, and in translation if appropriate;
- the community grapevine of organisations and workers;
- the media.

Parents who have been involved in family learning are good ambassadors. The London Language and Literacy Unit supports learners in their 'Families in Education Programme' to become advocates for the programme. As well as talking to other parents about the benefits, parents from the programme routinely speak to audiences of professionals about their experiences.

Facilitating family learning

The interactive stage of work with families is exciting but challenging. If there are two facilitators working with adults and children the need to co-ordinate efforts is another factor. Some of the main considerations are:

- choosing the best time and venue;
- welcoming families;
- negotiating the programme;
- creating a positive climate;
- promoting learning;
- assessing learning;
- recording progress;
- celebrating achievement;
- providing practical support for learners.

Table 2: Examples of national organisations offering programme development and support for family learning

Organisation	Focus	Programme
Basic Skills Agency (BSA)	Raising levels of attainment in basic skills in families	Family Literacy and Family Numeracy as well as shorter, more flexible programmes; family learning projects supported through Adult and Community Learning Fund
Book Trust	Reading in families	Administers Bookstart
Campaign for Learning	Families as settings for lifelong learning	Promotion of informal and formal learning through Family Learning Week-end and Family Learning At Work Day
Community Education Development Centre (CEDC)	Home-school-community relationships using community development context	SHARE, Fair Chance for Carers, It's a Man Thing, and other support for home-school partnerships
Education Extra	Family learning in study support contexts	Variety of study support models
Include	Families with a child at risk of exclusion	Primary Intervention Project
Kids Club Network	Supporting families through after school care	Out-of-school provision; support for 'centres for curiosity and discovery'
Liverpool Hope University and Liverpool City Council	empowerment for families and community	'REACHOut to Parents' offering progression routes from informal community based learning to degree level
NIACE	Families as settings for lifelong learning	Family learning projects supported through Adult and Community Learning Fund and related research and development programmes, including Family Learning
Open University	Families and lifelong learning	Confident Parents, Confident Children
Pre-School Learning Alliance (PSLA)	Care and education for families with pre-school children in community settings	Looking at Learning Together; management training for volunteer playgroup leaders; support for Family Learning Millennium projects
Workers' Educational Association (WEA)	Families as settings for lifelong learning	Helping in Schools, access courses for parents
YMCA	Fathers and sons learning together	Dads and Lads

An ideal venue is accessible to families, attractive, non-threatening, and adequate for the kinds of activities you plan to include. Every setting has advantages and disadvantages. For example, a school may be accessible but may have unpleasant associations for some parents. Where childcare is offered, the accommodation needs to be registered with Social Services. Access and security are important considerations in making people feel safe and welcomed.

The fundamental values of family learning should inform every interaction, from the first greeting through to the evaluation stage when learners reflect on what they have achieved. This is the case in CEDC's Share, a programme for parents who want to help their children at home (see case study, page 54).

Working collaboratively

The ideal of working collaboratively is central to family learning, though in reality it is not so easily achieved. As we saw in Chapter 5, Government policy enshrines the idea of parents as partners in home-school agreements. National initiatives such as Sure Start and New Deal for Communities frequently require individuals and organisations to form partnerships. Advice from Sure Start (page 55) includes guidance on partnerships.

At local level, collaborative working is formalised in a range of ways. Southend Adult Community College, for example, has developed a Family Learning Contract as the basis of joint working.

Regional family learning networks such as the West Midlands Family Learning Forum have been instrumental in addressing staff development needs and disseminating good practice widely.

Share – involving parents in children's learning

The programme is underpinned by respect for families' experience and recognition of parents as learners themselves.

Share works in three ways:

1. parents use attractively designed materials to support their children's learning;
2. children's learning at key stages 1, 2 and 3 in English and Maths is supported by activities carried out in the home and community;
3. the child's teacher works with a group of parents to help them to understand how children learn, the importance of their involvement and practical ways of making and using learning materials. This is usually an eye-opening experience for school staff and can act as a catalyst in changing the balance of power in home-school relationships.

Respect for parents and their ability to support learning are designed into Share. Share materials are high quality, conveying to parents that they are valued. Non-threatening learning projects give parents feedback on how their child learns, with results documented in activity books. Enjoying learning together is an important part of the experience. Learning activities for use at home are action-oriented and enable everyone to produce satisfying results. The evaluation of Share (Bastiani, 1999) noted how frequently the whole family gets involved in extended project work at home.

Teachers use an adult learning model in working with parents at school. Groupwork strategies are used to foster a climate of respect and mutual support. The ground rules which group members set at the outset guide the group's work. While working with adults in this way may present challenges for teachers initially, the evaluation shows that many become convinced of its effectiveness.

Share is accredited through the Open College Network, enabling many parents to gain recognition for their learning. In making the process of learning more transparent, Share helps parents to make the connection between their own learning and their child's.

(Funding Source: can be funded using a range of sources, including local authority, Standards Fund (Lifelong Learning), SRB, and charitable trusts.)

The experiences of Sure Start trailblazers suggest that three factors are critical to the success of a partnership:

▶ commitment: all the partners and their parent organisations must be prepared to make the effort to make the partnership work;

▶ unselfishness: the partners must use their expertise to benefit local children, not to promote the organisation;

▶ stability: partner members need to get to know and trust each other. Organisations should ensure that their representatives on Sure Start partnerships do not change without good reason.

(DfEE, 1999c)

Family learning policy

In most authorities partners have been focusing on developing new programmes and tapping into new opportunities for funding. Not surprisingly, Ofsted found that most family learning takes place in 'a policy vacuum' (Ofsted, 2000).

In many authorities policy is emerging from work at ground level. The first step in formalising a shared sense of purpose can be a family learning strategy. Many authorities include a family learning strategy in their Lifelong Learning Development Plans. These strategies prepare the groundwork for a formal policy.

A family learning policy should include:

▶ what family learning is and why it is important;
▶ values and principles;
▶ aims and objectives;
▶ the beneficiaries;
▶ the contribution of family learning to the corporate priorities;
▶ involvement of families in developing policy and practice;

Family Learning

1. Aim

To enhance the quality of family life through learning opportunities.

2. Principles

2.1 The diversity of family patterns in society is recognised and respected.

2.2 Opportunities for learning must be accessible to all families.

2.3 Recognition that learning within a family is inter-generational and unique.

2.4 Family learning spans a range of organisations and agencies that must work in partnership for effective delivery.

3. Objectives

3.1 To provide opportunities for parental learning for the benefit of children.

3.2 To provide opportunities to learn and develop parenting skills in partnership with others.

3.3 To provide opportunities for parents and children to play, learn and work together.

3.4 To identify local community needs and find responses through a multidisciplinary approach.

3.5 To support training opportunities for all those involved in the delivery of the family learning curriculum.

3.6 To identify problems of inequality and devise strategies which lead to their resolution.

3.7 To facilitate progression.

3.8 To promote lifelong learning with families.

(Somerset County Council, 1999)

- partners involved in supporting family learning;
- structures for supporting family learning;
- family learning provision;
- how provision is made;
- family learning priorities;
- resources for family learning;
- an action plan showing how aims and objectives will be met;
- provision for monitoring and evaluation;
- policy review process.

Family learning is one of five areas which make up the community education curriculum in Somerset. Aims and objectives for the area are set out in a policy statement, reproduced on page 56.

Ofsted (2000) encourages local authorities to recognise the contribution that family learning can make to a number of corporate priorities, such as social inclusion and raising achievement. Furthermore, Ofsted argues that policies should explain how resources will be targeted to ensure they reach groups where need is greatest.

At every level, from the neighbourhood to the national, a policy framework promotes clarity about the purpose of family learning and about how partners will work together to make it happen.

Key Points:

- consult with families in the community about their needs, using 'gatekeepers' as appropriate, and supplement this information with other data from your own records and that of other organisations;
- programme development, whatever the size of programme you have in mind, is a major investment in terms of energy, time and resources;
- the quality of relationships in family learning is critical in

encouraging families to take part and progress to further opportunities;

▶ providers should co-ordinate planning and delivery through a variety of collaborative agreements;

▶ family learning policy provides a framework for direction and purpose.

The Babelfish Project, Angel Row Gallery, Nottingham: exploring cultural identity with families *(encompass, involving families in gallery education)*

8

Funding family learning

Now that you and your partners have successfully developed some work on the ground and clarified the overall direction of your activities, you will need to seek the resources to make it sustainable.

This section examines the difficulties of using short-term funding to develop sustainable family learning provision. A summary of major funding sources is provided and the opportunities for further funding in the new post-16 era are noted.

Who pays for family learning?

Learning in families is resourced primarily by families themselves. There is, moreover, considerable inequality in what different families invest in learning. Inequality may be due to differences in material resources such as the money and the physical environment at families' disposal or to stressful factors they experience. It may also stem from the value that different families place on learning, influencing their allocation of time, attention and material resources.

Public and private resources can make a contribution to levelling up some of these inequalities by supporting families in difficult circumstances. For example, early intervention programmes such as Sure Start aim to ensure that no child starts school at a disadvantage. Additional resources can benefit every family, though, by valuing parents, promoting a culture of learning, and raising awareness of the opportunities to learn through family and community experiences.

There is no dedicated source of funding for family learning as it is not a statutory requirement.

A summary of public resources currently used for family learning is provided in Table 3 (pages 62 and 63). Each funding stream can provide some worthwhile elements of provision. The Standards Fund for Family Literacy and Family Numeracy has had a tremendous impact on family learning. It enables local authorities to provide the Basic Skills Agency (BSA) models in schools and community centres. Additional funds announced in 2000 will enable the BSA to fund demonstration projects aimed at encouraging new families to participate. The Single Regeneration Budget funds family learning which contributes to community regeneration. Birmingham's Core Skills Partnership is an excellent example of SRB funding which has enabled the city to take a strategic view of family learning. A significant proportion of the new second round of Education Action Zones features a family learning strand.

Sure Start and the Early Excellence Centres programme enable multi-agency partnerships to provide integrated services for families with young children. Families with children of all ages can be supported through study support and ICT learning centres funded through New Opportunities Fund. ESF brings additional funds to disadvantaged neighbourhoods and crucially can be used for childcare which is not fundable through other sources. Transnational European programmes enable families and staff in the UK to gain a new perspective on learning through exchanges of visits and strategies. The Family Learning Millennium Awards, funded through the national lottery between 1997 and 2000, were recognition of families' contribution to public life. The Pre-School Learning Alliance, which administers the fund, is particularly concerned to embed the projects to ensure that good work can be sustained when the funding ceases.

Most support for family learning is funded by pooling

Table 3 – Examples of possible sources for funding family learning

Name of funding body	Nature of activity	Additional comments	How to contact
Single Regeneration Budget (SRB)	Regeneration activities, e.g. ICT, Family Literacy.	Demonstrates family learning's contribution to community regeneration and social inclusion.	Regional Development Agency.
The Standards Fund	Family Literacy and Family Numeracy. Lifelong learning activities.	Has extended reach of FL and FN into schools and communities. Stimulated broader notion through Lifelong Learning Development Plan.	LEA Standards fund designated Officer or DfEE.
Home Office	Anti-crime. Community Safety Initiatives.	Not a specific fund.	Alert colleagues in Youth Justice or Chief Executive's Department to your interest.
DfEE Sure Start	Integrated services for 0 – 4 yrs.	By invitation of DfEE.	LEA Early Years Section
EU Socrates Fund Gruntvig	Exchange of good practice in adult education. Promotion of the European dimension.	Minimum of two transnational partners needed.	Bureau de Socrates el Jeunesse, 70 Rue Montoyer, Brussels B-0140, Belgium.

Table 3 *(continued)*

Name of funding body	Nature of activity	Additional comments	How to contact
Learning and Skills Council	Key areas: National Learning Targets, widening participation, basic skills.	Programmes fundable under national funding formula as well as others using discretionary budget.	www.dfee.gov.uk/post16 Local task groups preparing local plans; national and local LSCs to be operational from April 2001
TUC Learning Fund	Career development opportunities.	Funding family learning in basic skills.	DfEE
New Opportunities Fund (NOF)	Several strands: Out-of-school childcare, Community Access to Lifelong Learning, Healthy Living Centres.	Opportunities to weave family learning into community-based programmes.	www.nof.org.uk Dacre House, 19 Dacre Street, London, SW1H 0DH
New Deal	Community-based family learning with regeneration focus.	Has funded community research into family learning needs.	www.newdeal.gov.uk

resources from a number of different sources. Partnerships between public and voluntary sector organisations may bring several funding streams together. By pooling resources partners can achieve more than they can on their own. Until recently, for example, restrictions on FEFC funding meant it could only be used for accredited work. Furthermore, it can only fund programmes for those aged 16 and over. Other budgets have been used to provide the informal confidence-raising experiences which give families a taste for learning. The non-accredited experiences lead seamlessly into accredited provision, thus providing opportunities for progression.

Collaborative working is attractive to many funders, who are looking for evidence of 'joined-up' thinking and practice. The Tower Hamlets Family Learning Consortium, described below, identified the need for a development worker to carry forward the work that partners are developing collaboratively.

Local authorities have generally been lead players in family learning partnerships. Very few authorities, though, have a separate budget for family learning. In his survey of local authority family learning provision, McCormick (1999) found

---

London Borough of Tower Hamlets: Family Learning Consortium

The Working with Parents Consortium is an established multi-agency initiative in Tower Hamlets. It grew out of a successful multi-agency conference held in 1997 which demonstrated a clear need for better information about provision (both for providers and parents) and for a more co-ordinated approach to work with parents across the borough.

The consortium is run on an entirely voluntary basis and any income has to be self-generated. Collaboration has enabled the consortium to attract funding through the Single Regeneration Budget. From March 2000 a Development Worker will be funded to promote the consortium objectives.

(Funding Source: Single Regeneration Budget)

only a few local authorities which have made a long-term investment in family learning over the years. Authorities such as Liverpool, Coventry and Oxford have shown 'commitment and a considerable degree of vision' in protecting family learning when its contribution was not generally recognised. Now that it is, they enjoy a return on their investment in terms of good working relationships and well-developed programmes.

Even small amounts of ring-fenced budgets can have an impact in developing collaborative work and piloting models, as the Leicestershire County Council example demonstrates.

Why short-term funding is not adequate

The problems which arise from using multiple funding streams drawn primarily from external sources are well known. The funding tends to be short term and driven by quantifiable outputs. Developments which are just beginning to bear fruit can-

Leicestershire County Council: Quality Enhancement Fund

In 1999 a sum of £3,000 from the Education Department's Quality Enhancement Budget was ring-fenced for family learning initiatives. Leicestershire TEC matched the County Council's funds because it recognised the link between informal learning in families and training for the childcare workforce.

Providers were invited to submit proposals for developmental work. The response was very positive and while not every proposal could be funded, the Family Learning Network that grew out of the exercise was useful in sharing ideas and disseminating good practice.

The success of the first year persuaded both partners to invest more so that in only two years the fund has more than trebled and the range of new family learning models has grown. A relatively small budget has stimulated curriculum innovation and collaborative working.

not be sustained. If families and communities become cynical about the commitment of providers, the trust developed over time can be undermined. From a provider's point of view the amount of time spent seeking funding is considerable, often to little effect.

The need for a more secure framework for funding family learning is well recognised. Ofsted (2000) recommends that funding is earmarked at both local and national levels. It asks authorities to:

> 'consider earmarked funding for the development of family learning which moves beyond, although still importantly includes, the current focus on basic skills.'

Ofsted asks national government to 'make every effort to end the pattern of short-term funding' and to:

> 'consider earmarked central funding, through the Standards Fund, for broader family learning programmes than those solely concerned with literacy and numeracy.'

McCormick (1999) recommends that:

> 'part of the mainstream education budget, and certainly a share of the incremental growth in budgets for learning, should concentrate on joining up provision between the home and the school.'

Funding sustainable family learning

A 'manifesto for family learning' representing the views of key stakeholders calls for a 'long-term public funding framework which supports cross-sectoral partnership work for a broad range of integrated FL activities'. Funds would be drawn from:

▶ DfEE;
▶ other government departments;
▶ Learning and Skills Councils;

▶ employers through corporate tax incentives;
▶ tax incentives for families to learn.

(Campaign for Learning *et al*, 2000)

The role of Local Learning and Skills Councils is of considerable significance in creating a more stable funding environment. Family learning providers should now be communicating with their local Learning Partnerships, which are responsible for assessing need and consulting learners in their areas. The case for family learning should be made, highlighting its contribution to raising standards, social inclusion and widening participation.

Family learning should be supported through the LSC national funding formula where appropriate and through non-formula funding otherwise. This will provide a more secure funding base so that learning opportunities can be extended to reach more families and assure the quality of provision.

It is not yet clear how LSC funding and other funding streams, including that for schools, will come together, though guidance on such matters will no doubt start to appear soon. In the meantime, providers should be optimistic but careful to keep family learning on the funding agenda.

Key Points:

▶ there is no dedicated budget for family learning, but a number of budgets can support the work;
▶ short-term funding, which can prevent consolidation of family learning practice, should not be relied on to resource family learning;
▶ family learning providers need to ensure that their local Learning Partnerships understand the case for supporting family learning;
▶ Local Learning and Skills Councils, through both formula funding and non-formula funding, will play a central role in ensuring the long-term future of family learning.

Making time to support lifelong learning *(Fela Adebiyi)*

9

Quality

Once programmes are underway and funding has been secured, you will want to ensure that the quality of provision is good. Quality assurance guarantees accountability to both funders and learners. This section looks at three aspects of quality assurance:

▶ standards for family learning;
▶ quality assurance procedures;
▶ staff development and training.

Which model?

Quality assurance in family learning is an under-developed area. Ofsted (2000) comments on the 'absence of a satisfactory quality assurance system for the full range of family learning' in the provision it inspected.

A quality assurance system needs to take account of the particular context of family learning. Family learning programmes which are part of large national initiatives, such as Sure Start and the BSA's Family Literacy and Family Numeracy programmes, will be guided by a national quality assurance strategy. All Sure Start programmes have national targets to meet and will use a nationally devised, IT-based performance monitoring system. Family learning which is part of Single Regeneration Budget or New Deal programmes will be expected to use their quality assurance systems.

A local quality assurance strategy for family learning should be flexible enough to adapt to the wide range of settings in which provision occurs, while robust enough to ensure that users everywhere receive the same minimum entitlement of service. This entails:

▶ identifing quality standards and quality indicators;
▶ monitoring and evaluation procedures;
▶ a strategy for developing quality in staff.

Quality standards and indicators

There are as yet no national standards and quality indicators in family learning. In the absence of national standards, providers adopt existing standards from a range of related areas, including:

▶ adult education;
▶ early years;
▶ youth and community work.

Most local authorities have quality descriptors for adult education, youth and community work services based on Ofsted frameworks for adult and community education and for schools. Ofsted's recent inspection of family learning (Ofsted, 2000) was a joint exercise between its Post-Compulsory Education and Primary and Nursery Divisions, each using the relevant Ofsted standards. Their definition of family learning, 'learning which brings together different family members to work on a common theme for some, if not the whole, of a planned programme' is, however, narrower than the scope of family learning currently provided.

Most authorities have produced standards for work in early years, including standards relating to work with parents and the community. Standards relating to the involvement of parents in schools are particularly well developed in local authority school self-evaluation strategies (Bastiani, 2000b).

A major national initiative will soon be underway to identify occupational standards for those working in parent education and support. The Parenting Education and Support Forum (PESF) and PAULO, the recently established National Training Organisation for community-based learning and development, will jointly manage a project which will:

▶ identify the sector and its stakeholders;
▶ prepare an occupational and functional map;
▶ identify existing occupational standards appropriate to the parenting education and support sector.

Use of an External Consultant to Pilot Standards in the Quality of Teaching

Calderdale Adult Education was one of the authorities visited by HM Inspectors during Ofsted's survey of family learning. As a result of the visit, they decided to address issues around the quality of teaching. They used DfEE funding made available to all local authorities in 1999 to appoint an external consultant to carry out the work.

The consultant drew up a list of quality indicators for teaching family learning and produced a pro-forma for observing family learning sessions. Each tutor was observed teaching, and the results of the sessions analysed to identify weaknesses in the service. This produced an agenda for in-service training in three areas:

▶ setting of objectives;
▶ planning lessons;
▶ evidence of early literacy skills.

Following the training session, individual feedback sessions were offered, and taken up by most of the tutors.

There were many benefits in terms of staff development. Tutors found the in-service training useful and particularly enjoyed sharing ideas with colleagues. There was a unanimous request for further sessions and opportunities for staff to meet and exchange ideas. Tutors also appreciated the individual feedback.

Consulting Stakeholders on the Success Criteria for Family Learning

Bristol Community Education is approaching standard setting as part of a much broader initiative in community consultation. The service is committed to a bottom-up approach to community consultation to inform its planning for regeneration proposals and other community initiatives. Family learning is at the heart of many of Bristol's regeneration programmes.

Local people are trained in community research and employed to undertake the research. This is what two women say about being a community researcher:

'I am a resident in the New Deal area…I am a refugee and I am a Somali woman…Schools do not understand our children's needs and do not spend enough time talking to us parents. I need to solve this problem of our children's religious needs in school. I heard about the Parent Consultation Group and I wanted to do it, so that is why I joined the group.'

'I became involved in New Deal after seeing an ad in their newsletter asking for people to interview parents, teachers and children about what they would like in their schools. I do not want our children to miss out on this opportunity that could change things for the better in our community.'

(New Deal for Communities Bristol, n.d.)

As the evidence about what stakeholders want from family learning builds up, a model of family learning standards is beginning to emerge. Though still in a very early stage, the standards embrace the priorities and expectations of the communities involved. For example, a quality indicator for 'recruitment' is that parents are involved in the recruitment of others.

(Source of Funding: New Deal for Communities)

Meanwhile authorities are beginning to identify their own standards for family learning, using a range of approaches, Calderdale's teaching standards are described on page 71.

The Community Education Service in Bristol is using its community research initiative, described on page 72, to generate standards.

Monitoring and evaluation

Evaluation enables us to make judgements about the value of the provision. Monitoring processes are needed to collect the evidence upon which valid and reliable judgements can be made.

Bastiani (1999) identifies the key elements of a practical evaluation strategy:

▶ a mixture of planned activities and positive opportunism (you just never know what's going to turn up);
▶ a continuous task, rather than one left until the end of the year (it's too late to do a lot of things then anyway!);
▶ minimal disruption and maximum usefulness;
▶ a combination of different kinds of data (don't put all your eggs in one basket!);
▶ an integral part of the professional mind-set, rooted in everyday practice.

This common-sense approach can help to embed evaluation in routine practices.

The first step is being clear about the aims of the family learning programme and deciding what would count as evidence of success in achieving those aims. Despite the fact that most programmes aim to develop confidence and other social benefits, the measures of success are generally expressed in quantitative performance indicators (Ofsted, 2000). Quantitative indicators for family learning, for example, are set out in Somerset County Council's Lifelong Learning Development Plan:

▶ participation rates: the total number of families taking part;
▶ range of activities: the number of activities being offered;
▶ widening participation: the number of families from selected postcodes;
▶ inter-agency working: the percentage of joint activities;
▶ progression: the number of adult family members moving into adult education provision.

(Somerset County Council, 1999)

In evaluating the Share programme of parental involvement, Bastiani (1999) considers a wide range of evidence, including:

▶ formal grades and scores (derived from established classroom practice);
▶ the judgements of teachers;
▶ the views of parents;
▶ children's work and comments.

He looks at the work parents and children produce, including parents' diaries if available and children's work at home:

'Parents' diaries, in particular, have provided a picture of work in home settings which would otherwise be invisible and inaccessible.' (Bastiani, 1999)

Qualitative indicators capturing the social and personal benefits of family learning could include:

▶ enhanced confidence of parents;
▶ enhanced confidence of children;
▶ children's attitudes to school;
▶ parents' attitudes to school;
▶ family cohesion;
▶ improved ability of parents to cope;
▶ enhanced participation in community life.

The development of tools to measure these benefits is an important challenge for practitioners and managers.

You will need to establish systems for collecting information to help you make judgements about your success. It is useful to collect data about:

► learners (age, gender, ethnicity, address, previous learning, goals);
► learning processes and outcomes (programme outlines, plans);
► assessment of learners' progress;
► teaching;
► learners' views;
► teachers' views;
► learners' achievements;
► destinations of learners.

The Boots Company Family Learning Project: a study support initiative with Education Extra

The aims of the initiative are to raise standards of achievement and to enhance self esteem through family learning. Other aims are spin-offs for the design and technology curriculum and an innovative educational partnership involving business. Sponsored by the Boots Company and supported by Education Extra, it is delivered in schools in targeted areas of Nottingham.

Monitoring systems are deliberately unobtrusive so that the trust that is developing between schools and families is not damaged. There is no enrolment as such, though workshop leaders keep records of family members attending each session. Collecting information on attendance is a considerable feat when as many as 60 adults and children are engaged in active design and technology project work.

'Family passports', complete with a photograph, are kept by families to record their progress throughout the programme. Passports are stamped when families complete the projects. Photographs of project work are taken freely throughout the sessions to build up a record of children's and adults' growing confidence.

(Funding: Financial commitment from The Boots Company, with support from Education Extra and individual schools)

The manner in which the information is collected, however, depends very much on the context, as the example om page 75 demonstrates.

Most authorities have other ways of evaluating family learning provision through, for example:

▶ classroom observation;
▶ the use of external consultants;
▶ internal inspection/review;
▶ Best Value review.

Stockton Adult Education Service, for example, assembled a team of specialist inspectors, including several from outside the service, to look at family learning across the borough.

External evaluations are making a considerable contribution to the evidence base for family learning. The Basic Skills Agency, in particular, has built up a solid base of evidence for the effectiveness of its Family Literacy and Family Numeracy programmes.

In general, providers recognise that a more systematic approach to quality assurance is needed in order to demonstrate the long-term gains of family learning.

Staff development and training

The development of family learning provision, where learners of different ages are working together, has produced a range of new staff roles. The notion of linking home and school underpins many of these roles, such as Coventry's team of dedicated Home School Teachers. The London Language and Literacy Unit enables parents to progress from informal learning through accredited learning to become facilitators, with a distinctive role in the neighbourhood. Many providers, for example the Pre-School Learning Alliance, are instrumental in encouraging parents to train as group facilitators, where their experience and skill in establishing relationships with other parents are valued.

The AMBER Project in Nottingham puts Parent Education Support Workers (PESW) in primary schools to work with mainly Asian and Afro-Caribbean parents. Their role is to provide encouragement and practical advice for parents to support their children's education, as well as to promote adults' own learning. The knowledge and skills needed for the role is wide-ranging, drawing upon community development, home-school liaison, adult education, ESOL and basic skills. The project has given local parents from minority communities the opportunity to gain valuable training and work experience.

Family learning presents distinctive staff development issues. Staff are frequently recruited with specialist knowledge of either adult or children's learning. 'There is a lack, in most instances, however, of staff whose qualifications and experience enable them to function easily in all phases and across all sectors' (Ofsted, 2000). On the other hand, a team teaching approach requires a considerable 'balancing act of diverse, sometimes conflicting , needs and complementary approaches' from two specialists from different backgrounds. Team teaching and team building are especially important as the relationships within family learning staff teams will affect relationships in general.

Key Points:

- assuring the quality of family learning provision is a key challenge for the future;
- starting on issues that directly involve families and staff and working in ways that draw on their experience will be more effective than overly bureaucratic approaches to quality;
- the development of a skilled and committed staff is central to the quality of family learning.

Laing Art Gallery, Newcastle: inviting families to use their imagination
(*Kids Club Network, centres for curiosity & imagination*)

Part 4

Conclusion

This section takes stock of where we are in family learning and looks at ways of moving forward. The challenges ahead are great, but so are the opportunities.

Family learning – an investment for the future *(Fela Adebiyi)*

10

Moving forward

The multitude of family learning patterns highlighted in the previous chapters might seem almost overwhelming. It is useful now to pause, stand back and get some perspective on what we have seen.

Looking back

Family learning has been taking shape fairly quietly on the margins of adult education, school improvement, early years and basic skills. It has been emerging from the spaces between the big set pieces such as the national literacy and numeracy strategies.

There has been no shortage of innovation in programme development, nor in staff commitment to making family learning happen locally on the ground. Particularly inventive has been its ability to spread relatively small amounts of resource over a large area. As Part Two of the guide demonstrates, well-defined approaches to family learning have been developed.

However, the portrayal of the wider benefits of family learning through systematic evaluation, including that over a long-term period, has been absent. The evaluations of Family Literacy by the National Foundation for Educational Research for the Basic Skills Agency are a notable exception. Evaluations of the Bookstart initiative and CEDC's Share programme are likewise valuable.

Where we stand now

Family learning as a notion is widely recognised now, though some lack of clarity persists about its scope. It is no longer viewed exclusively as a tool for raising educational achievement, but also for the contribution it can make to social inclusion, community regeneration, and the economy.

This phase is about the consolidation of good practice that has developed so far. Evaluation and programme review will help to make good provision more sustainable. Providers and managers at local level need to evaluate programmes more systematically to produce reliable and valid evidence about family learning. Evaluations of new national programmes will, in time, make a valuable contribution to the evidence base for family learning.

Additional resources coming into family learning through national initiatives like Sure Start, Early Excellence Centres and Family Literacy and Family Numeracy, are welcomed. It is not yet clear, though, how the breadth of curriculum that is developing can be sustained without a commitment to long-term funding.

Where next?

The picture emerging is one in which family learning is steadily gaining legitimacy. The image is not yet sharp, and even as it appears, the gound is moving. The new Learning and Skills Council appears large on the horizon and the frenetic pace of change continues. The creativity, industry and good humour that have characterised family learning so far will be needed just as much, or more, in the future.

The impact, though, that family learning is making now will leave an impression on learners for years to come.

Useful Contacts

Organisation	Address	Telephone number	Fax number	e-mail
Basic Skills Agency	Commonwealth House, 1-19 New Oxford Street, London, WC1A 1NU	020 7405 4017	020 7440 6626	enquiries@ basic-skills.co.uk
Book Trust	Book House, 45 East Hill, London, SW18 2QZ	020 8516 2977	020 8516 2978	booktrust@ dial.pipex.com
Campaign for Learning	19 Buckingham Street, London, WC2N 6EF	020 7930 1111	020 7930 1551	tgreany@ cflearning.org.uk
Campaign for Learning in Museums and Galleries	The Old Ship, Fore Street, Stratton, Cornwall, EX23 9DA	01288 354536	01288 359 363	Nicola-Nuttall@ msn.com
Community Education Development Council	Woodway Park School, Wigston Road, Coventry, CV2 2RH	01203 6557000	01203 655 702	info@cedc.org.uk
Contact a Family	170 Tottenham Court Road, London, W1P 0HA	020 7383 3555	020 7383 0259	info@ cafamily.org.uk
DfEE	Head Office, Sanctuary Buildings, Great Smith Street, Westminster, London, SW1P 3BT	020 7925 5000	020 7925 6000	
DfEE Publications	Sherwood Park, Annesley, Nottingham, NG15 0DJ	0845 602 2260	0845 603 3360	dfee@ prologistics.co.uk
Education Extra	St Margaret's House, 17 Old Ford Road, Bethnal Green, London, E2 9PL	020 89831061		
Encompass	4 Hebron Road,	0117 907 0234	0117 907 0247	Gilnicol@

Organisation	Bristol, BS3 3AB Address	Telephone number	Fax number	dircon.co.uk e-mail
Family Caring Trust	44 Rathfriland Road, Newry, Co Down, BT34 ILD	01693 64174		
Family Policy Studies Centre	9 Tavistock Place, London, WC1H 9SN	020 7388 5900	020 7388 5600	fpsc@ mailbox.ulcc.ac.uk
Include	8 High Street, Ely, Cambs, CB7 4JY	01353 650 350	01351 650 450	enquiries@ include.org.uk
Kids Clubs Network UK	Bellerive House, 3, Muirfield Crescent, London, E14 9S2	020 7512 2112	020 0751 2010	toniaia.sutton@ kidsclubs.co.uk
National Family and Parenting Institute	53-79 Highgate Road, London, NW5	0207 424 3466		
Parenting Education and Support Forum	Unit 43, 53-79 Highgate Road, London, NW5	020 7284 8380		
Parentline Plus	520 Highgate Studios, 53-79 Highgate Road, Kentish Town, London, NW5 1TL	020 7284 5500	020 7284 5501	centraloffice@ parentlineplus.org.uk
Pre-School Learning Alliance	69 Kings Cross Road, London, WC1X 9LL	020 7833 0991	020 7837 4942	pla@ pre-school.org.uk
WEA	Temple House, 17 Victoria Park Square, London, E2 9PB	020 8983 1515	020 8983 4840	info@ wea.org.uk
Working with Men	320 Commercial Way, London, SE15 1QN	0207 732 9409		
YMCA England Parenting and Education Support	25-27 Dee Bridge House, Chester, CH1 1RS	01244 403 090	01244 315 108	dirk@parenting. ymca.org.uk

Bibliography

Adult literacy and Basic Skills Unit (1993) *Parents and their Children: the intergenerational effect of poor basic skills*, Century.

Alexander, T. (1997) *Family Learning: The Foundation of Effective Education*, Demos.

Alexander, T. and Clyne, P. (1995) *Riches Beyond Price: Making the Most of Family Learning*, NIACE.

Baker, K. and Baldwin, P (1999) *Making the Links: Early Years to Lifelong Learning*, The Education Network.

Ball, M. (1998) *School Inclusion: The School, the Family and the Community*, Joseph Rowntree Foundation.

Basic Skills Agency (1997) *It Doesn't Get Any Better: the Impact of Poor Basic Skills on the Lives of 37 Year Olds.* Summary of the Main Findings, Basic Skills Agency.

Basic Skills Agency (1999) *Family Numeracy Adds Up*, Basic Skills Agency.

Basic Skills Agency (1999) *Family Literacy 2000–2001: Guidance for LEAs on Key Features.* Basic Skills Agency.

Basic Skills Agency (1999) *Family Numeracy 2000–2001: Guidance for LEAs on Key Features.* Basic Skills Agency.

Bastiani, J. (ed.) (1997) *Home-School Work in Multicultural Settings*, David Fulton Publishers.

Bastiani, J. (1999) *Share: An Evaluation of the First Two Years*, CEDC.

Bastiani, J. (2000a) *The Amber Project: a formative evaluation.* (draft version) Nottingham Black Initiative, unpublished.

Bastiani, J. (2000b) I know it works!…Actually proving it is the problem! in S. Wolfendale and J. Bastiani (eds) *The Contribution of Parents to School Effectiveness*, David Fulton.

Bentley, T. (1998) *Learning Beyond the Classroom: Education for a Changing World*, Routledge.

Bernardes, J. (1999) *Family Studies: An Introduction*, Routledge.

Brooks, G., Gorman, T., Harman, J., Hutchison, D., and Wilkin, A. (1996) *Family Literacy Works: The NFER Evaluation of the Basic Skills Agency's Family Literacy Demonstration Programmes*, Basic Skills Agency.

Brooks, G., Gorman, T., Harman, J., Hutchison, D., Kinder, K., Moor, H. and Wilkin, A. (1997) *Family Literacy Lasts: The NFER Follow-up Study of the Basic Skills Agency's Demonstration Programmes*, Basic Skills Agency.

Brooks, G., Harman, J., Hutchison, D., Kendall. S. and Wilkin, A. (1999) *Family Literacy for New Groups: The NFER Evaluation of Family Literacy with Linguistic Minorities, Year 4 and Year 7*, Basic Skills Agency.

Bufftton, J. (1999) *Family Learning: Taking the Work Forward*, Working Paper of the National Advisory Group for Continuing Education and Lifelong Learning, unpublished.

Campaign for Learning NIACE, Scottish Council Foundation, CEDC, Education Extra (2000) *A Manifesto for Family Learning*. Campaign for Learning.

Capper, L. (1998) *Parents as Educators in Europe*, CEDC.

Capper, L., Downes, P. and Jenkinson, D. (1998) *Successful Schools: Parental Involvement in Secondary Schools*, CEDC.

Capper, L. (2000) '"Am I doing it right?" Share – a national parental involvement programme' in S. Wolfendale and J. Bastiani (eds) *The Contribution of Parents to School Effectiveness*, David Fulton.

Carter, R. (1998) *Mapping the Mind*, Weidenfield and Nicolson.

Clark, R. (1983) *Family Life and School Achievement: Why Poor Black Children Succeed or Fail*, Chicago University Press.

Cusick, J. (2000) *Working with Parents in the Youth Justice Context*, Trust for the Study of Adolescence.

Dex, S. (ed) (1999) *Families and the Labour Market: Trends, Pressures, Policies*, Family Policies Studies Centre.

DfEE (1997) *Excellence in Schools*, Cm 3681, HMSO.

DfEE (1998) *Meeting the Childcare Challenge*, Cm 3959, HMSO.

DfEE (1999a) *Extending opportunity: a national framework for study support*, DfEE.

DfEE (1999b) *A fresh start: Improving literacy and numeracy* (The report of the working group chaired by Sir Claus Moser), DfEE.

DfEE (1999c) *Sure Start: A guide for second-wave programmes*, DfEE.

Dyson, A. and Robson, E. (1999) *School, Family, Community: Mapping School Inclusion in the UK*, Youth Work Press and Joseph Rowntree Foundation.

Ferri, E. and Smith, K. (1996) *Parenting in the 1990s*, Family Policy Studies Centre.

Goleman, D. (1996) *Emotional Intelligence: Why it can matter more than IQ*, Bloomsbury.

Gloucestershire County Council.(1998) *Family Learning Curriculum Review*, unpublished.

Greenfield, S. (1996) *The Human Mind Explained*, Cassell.

Grimshaw, R. and McGuire, C. (1998) *Evaluating Parenting Programmes: A Study of Stakeholders' Views*, National Children's Bureau.

Hannon, P. (1995) *Literacy, Home and School*, The Falmer Press.

Herbert, G. and Napper, R.(2000) *Tried and Tested Ideas for Parent Education and Support*, Oxfordshire County Council Professional, Personal and Organisational Development Service.

Home Office (1998) *Supporting Families: A Consultation Document*, HMSO.

Leadbeater, C. and Christie, C. (1999) *To Our Mutual Advantage*, Demos.

Lewis, C. (2000) *A Man's Place Is In the Home: Fathers and Families in the U.K*, Joseph Rowntree Foundation.

McCormick, J. (1999) *Family Learning: Parents as Co-Educators*, The Scottish Council Foundation.

McGivney, V. (1999a) *Excluded Men: Men Who Are Missing from Education and Training*, NIACE.

McGivney, V. (1999b) *Informal Learning in the Community*, NIACE.

McGivney, V. (2000) *Pre-School: The Contribution of Pre-Schools to the Community*, Pre-School Learning Alliance.

Millard, E. (2000) *It's a Man Thing! Draft Evaluation*, CEDC, unpublished.

Moss, P. (1996) 'Increasing Men's Involvement with their Children' in T. Lloyd and T. Wood (eds) *What Next For Men?*, Working with Men.

Moss, P. and Poland, G. (1999) *Re-thinking School: Some International Perspectives*, Youth Work Press.

Mufti, E. (1999) *Summary Document of Research Carried Out on the REACHOut to Parents, Our Family Matters Module*, Liverpool Hope University College, unpublished.

NCH Action for Children (1997) *Family Life: the Age of Anxiety*, NCH Action for Children.

New Deal for Communities Bristol (n.d.) *Families, Fun and School*, New Deal for Communities Bristol.

NFER (2000) *Evaluation of Share: A Fair Chance*, Draft evaluation of programme for carers, CEDC, unpublished.

OECD Centre for Educational Research and Innovation (1997) *Parents as Partners in Schooling*, OECD.

OECD Centre for Educational Research and Innovation (1999) *Overcoming Exclusion Through Adult Learning*, OECD.

Ofsted (2000) *Family Learning: A Survey of Current Practice*, HMSO.

Oxfordshire County Council, (1999) *Learning Forever, Lifelong Learning, Development Plan (2000-03)*, Oxfordshire County Council, unpublished.

'Parenting in Plymouth' in News Bulletin Number 3, August 2000, Parenting Education and Support Forum.

Parsons, C. and Bynner, J. (2000) *Basic Skills and Social Exclusion*, Basic Skills Agency (in press).

Pascal, C., Bertram, T., Gasper, M., Mould, C., Ramsden, F. and Saunders, M. (1999) *Research to Inform the Evaluation of the Early Excellence Centres Pilot Programme*, Centre for Research in Early Childhood, University College Worcester.

Pen Green Centre for under 5s and their families (n.d.) 'A Curriculum Document for Parents and Children'. Pen Green Centre for under 5's and their families, unpublished.

Policy Action Team on Skills (1999) *Skills for Neighbourhood Renewal: Local Solutions*, DfEE.

Pugh, G. De'Ath, E. and Smith, C. (1994) *Confident Parents, Confident Children*, National Children's Bureau.

Ramsay, N. (2000) 'Thinking in the Future Tense' in H. Wilkinson (ed), *Family Business*, Demos.

Schools Plus Policy Action Team (2000) *Schools Plus: Building Learning Communities (Improving the Education Chances of Children and Young People from Disadvantaged Areas)*, DfEE.

Skolnick, A. (2000) 'A Time of Transition' in H.Wilkinson, (ed) *Family Business*, Demos.

Social Exclusion Unit (1998) *Bringing Britain Together: A National Strategy for Neighbourhood Renewal*, The Stationery Office.

Social Exclusion Unit (2000) *National Strategy for Neighbourhood Renewal: a framework for consultation*, The Stationery Office.

Somerset County Council (1999) *Local Authority Lifelong Learning Development Plan*, unpublished.

Tizard, B. and Hughes, M. (1984) *Young Children Learning: Talking and Thinking at Home and in School*, Fontana.

Thompson, J. (2000) *Social Exclusion: NIACE Briefing Sheet 10*, NIACE

Wade, B. and Moore, M. (2000) 'Starting Early with Books' in Wolfendale and Bastiani (eds) *The Contribution of Parents to School Effectiveness*, David Fulton Publishers.

Walton, M. (1998) *Family Literacy and Learning*, Folens Ltd. Publishers

Warin, J., Solomon, Y., Lewis, C. and Langford, W. (1999) *Fathers, Work and Family Life*, Family Policy Studies Centre.

Whalley, M. (1994) *Learning to be Strong: Setting Up a Neighbourhood Service for Under-Fives and Their Families*, Hodden and Stoughton.

Whalley, M. and the Pen Green Centre Team (1997) *Working with Parents*, Hodden and Stoughton.

Whalley, M. and the Pen Green Centre Team (1998) *Parents' Involvement in their Children's Learning: End of Year Report, April 1997 – March 1998*, Pen Green Centre for under 5s and their families. unpublished.

Whalley, M. and the Pen Green Centre Team (1999) *Parents' Involvement in their Children's Learning: Interim Report April 1998 – March 1999*, Pen Green Centre for under 5s and their families. unpublished.

Wilkinson, H. (ed.) (2000) *Family Business*, Demos.

Wolfendale, S. and Bastiani, J.(eds) (2000) *The Contribution of Parents to School Effectiveness*, David Fulton.

Family Learning Advisory Group

Fiona Aldridge, NIACE

Titus Alexander, Learning Initiatives

Maureen Banbury, OFSTED

Sue Barnes, Leicester Education Action Zone

Jean Brook, Middlesbrorough Adult Education Service

Jacqui Bufffton, Consultant

Lisa Capper, CEDC

Mary Crowley, The Parenting Education and Support Forum

Pauline Henniker, Pre-School Learning Alliance

Sue Houlton, Leicestershire County Council

Phillipa Langton, WEA

Catherine McPartland, Open College Network (Teesside Valley, Wearside and Cumbria)

Annie Merton, NIACE

Alwyn Morgan, Alwyn Morgan and Associates

Sian Welby, Basic Skills Agency

Linda Wright, Croydon Continuing Education and Training Service